Treatment Strategies for Abused Children

Activity Book for
Treatment Strategies for Abused Children

From Victim to Survivor

Cheryl L. Karp
Traci L. Butler

Interpersonal Violence:
The Practice Series

SAGE Publications
International Educational and Professional Publisher
Thousand Oaks   London   New Delhi

For information address:

 SAGE Publications, Inc.
2455 Teller Road
Thousand Oaks, California 91320
E-mail: order@sagepub.com

SAGE Publications Ltd.
6 Bonhill Street
London EC2A 4PU
United Kingdom

SAGE Publications India Pvt. Ltd.
M-32 Market
Greater Kailash I
New Delhi 110 048 India

Printed in the United States of America

Library of Congress Cataloging-in-Publication Data

Karp, Cheryl L.
    Treatment strategies for abused children from victim to survivor /
authors, Cheryl L. Karp, Traci L. Butler.
        p. cm.—(Interpersonal violence: the practice series; v. 13)
    Includes bibliographical references and index.
    ISBN 0-8039-7217-2 (acid-free paper)—ISBN 0-8039-7218-0
(pbk.: acid-free paper).
    1. Abused children—Rehabilitation. 2. Sexually abused children—
Rehabilitation. 3. Child psychotherapy. I. Butler, Traci L. II. Title.
III. Series: Interpersonal violence; v. 13.
RJ507.A29K37   1996
618.92'85822303—dc20   96-4425

This book is printed on acid-free paper.

99 10 9 8 7

Sage Production Editor: Michèle Lingre
Sage Typesetter: Janelle LeMaster

Contents

PHASE II: EXPLORATION OF TRAUMA

PHASE III: REPAIRING THE SENSE OF SELF

PHASE IV: BECOMING FUTURE ORIENTED

1

Stages of Sexual Development

❑ **Preschool (0 - 4 Years)**

NORMAL SIGNS

- Intense curiosity about the world around them and about their bodies.
- Masturbation normally begins in early infancy and continues through the preschool years as a self-soothing behavior—generally not discreet.
- Interested in looking at others' bodies. Children aged 2 and 3 are especially interested in the bathroom activity of others.
- Preschoolers will take advantage of opportunities to touch others' genitalia if permitted or allowed to.
- Take redirection quickly and respond positively to limit-setting about touching others' bodies.
- Touching is of an exploratory rather than a coercive nature and is mostly "imitative."

"ABNORMAL" SIGNS

- When curiosity becomes obsessive preoccupation.
- When exploration becomes reenactment of specific adult activity.
- When children's behavior involves coercion toward others or injury to themselves.

❏ **Young School Age (5 - 7 Years)**

NORMAL SIGNS

- Continue to touch and fondle their own genitals, evolving into masturbation.
- Become more secretive about their self-touching and in a less random way.
- Discover creative ways of masturbating.
- Interest in viewing others' bodies continues although it changes from "curiosity seeking" to more "game playing."
- Games such as "I'll show you mine, you show me yours" and "doctor" continues.
- Ask questions such as, "where did I come from?"
- Interested in pictures of the human body, and may giggle a great deal when they see people kissing on TV—both "grossed-out" and fascinated.
- Feelings of needing privacy emerge at this age.
- Touching others' genitalia usually takes place in a game-like atmosphere and involves stroking or rubbing.

"ABNORMAL" SIGNS

- Sexual penetration.
- Genital kissing or oral copulation.
- Simulated intercourse.
- "Coercive" sex-play.

❏ Latency-Aged Children (7 - 12 Years)

NORMAL SIGNS

- Masturbation continues as a sexual behavior for latency-aged children.
- They may have alternating periods of disinhibition and inhibition.
- At ages 9 and 10, begin seeking information about sex and looks for books and diagrams that explain their own organs and functions.
- Puberty: Boys—develop pubic hair and the ability to masturbate to ejaculation:
    Girls—may develop pubic hair, breasts, and begin their menses.
- Swearing begins during this stage, and young boys develop certain locker-room behavior—telling dirty jokes and having "ejaculation contests."
- Girls also have locker room behavior that may include comparing breast sizes and experimenting with varying degrees of nudity.
- Many preadolescents "fall in love" and engage in sexual activity with peers, including

    — open-mouth kissing, sexual fondling, simulated intercourse, sexual penetration behaviors, and intercourse.

- Most experiences are heterosexual, however, it is common for preadolescents to have some same-gender sexual experiences.
- There may be intense interest in viewing others' bodies, especially members of the opposite sex.

    — This may take the form of looking at photographs or published material, including pornography.

"ABNORMAL" SIGNS

- It is highly unusual for 7- to 10-year-old children to engage in sexual penetration, genital kissing, or oral copulation.
- It is highly unusual for preadolescents (10 - 12 years) and adolescents to become involved in sexual play with younger children.
- Coercive, exploitative, or aggressive sexual behavior is considered abnormal behavior for all age groups.

PHASE I

Establishing
Therapeutic Rapport

2

Who Am I?
Image Building, Goal Setting,
and Therapeutic Trust

❑ **Message to the Kids**

Kids who are using the activities in this book have been emotionally, physically, and/or sexually abused. You, like the other kids who are working through this book, will be learning about yourself and your feelings. You will be able to better understand how your abuse makes you feel today and learn more helpful ways of taking care of yourself.

Kids who have been hurt use many different ways of trying to take care of their feelings instead of talking about their feelings. Sometimes they push their feelings down so that they don't have to feel them, hurt other people because they are hurting, say they don't have any feelings, or eat lots of food to try to make their insides feel better. How do you take care of your feelings?

The first step in taking care of your feelings is to share more about you and your family and to begin setting goals. This chapter has many activities for you to do so you can begin your journey of becoming the best you. Good luck!

❏ **Activity #1: All About Me!**

My name is _____ .

I am _____ years old. My birthdate is _____ .

I have _____ hair. I am_____ inches tall.

I am in the _____ grade.

My school is _____ .

My teacher's name is _____ .

I live with _____

_____ .

My mom's name is _____ .

My dad's name is _____ .

I have _____ brothers and _____ sisters.

Their names (and ages) are: _____

_____

_____

_____

I am/am not happy with my family. (Circle one)

Things I like to do: _____

_____

_____

_____

_____

Other things that I think are important to know about me are: _____

_____

_____

_____

_____

My pets and their names are: _____

_____

_____

My best friend is _____ .

❏ **Activity #2: Me!**

• Draw a picture of yourself.

❏ **Activity #3: My Family**

• Draw a picture of your family.

❑ **Activity #4: Family Activity**

• Draw a picture of your family doing something together.

❑ **Activity #5: My Animal Family**

- Draw a picture of each family member as an animal.

❏ Activity #6: My Three Wishes

- Write or draw your three wishes.

❑　**Activity #8: The Looking Glass**

- Look in a mirror and draw a picture of what you see.

❑ **Activity #9: I Like Me Because . . .**

• Write down five things you like about yourself.

1. _____

    _____

    _____

2. _____

    _____

    _____

3. _____

    _____

    _____

4. _____

    _____

    _____

5. _____

    _____

    _____

❏ **Activity #10: My Goals**

• Write down five things you would like to change about yourself.

1. _____

   _____

   _____

2. _____

   _____

   _____

3. _____

   _____

   _____

4. _____

   _____

   _____

5. _____

   _____

   _____

3

Feelings

Everyone has feelings. A lot of times people will call feelings either good or bad, but a feeling is really just a feeling. All feelings are okay. Your feelings may come from different experiences. What you see, hear, touch, smell, and sometimes what you taste may bring back thoughts and feelings from your past experiences.

Sometimes kids who have been abused learn to *stuff* or put their feelings away so they don't have to feel them. The problem with stuffing your feelings is that it makes it hard to tell someone else how you feel.

This chapter is to help you learn how to label your different feelings so that you can let others know how you feel. You also will learn how to use your words so that others will be able to listen and understand you.

❑ **Activity #11: Feelings Chart**

• Draw a face for each feeling on the chart.

HAPPY	**SAD**
FRUSTRATED	**SCARED**
ANGRY	**PROUD**

❏ **Activity #12: How Would You Feel?**

- Write about your feelings as if you are in the following situations.

  1. Sally was invited to spend the night at her best friend's house.

  _____

  _____

  _____

  _____

  2. Jennifer raised her hand, but the teacher never called on her.

  _____

  _____

  _____

  _____

  3. Brian woke up in the middle of the night because he heard a strange noise.

  _____

  _____

  _____

  _____

  4. José got in line first, but Freddy cut in front of him.

  _____

  _____

  _____

  _____

❏ **Activity #13: My Feelings**

- Share your feelings by completing the following "I feel" statements.

1. I feel happy when _____

   _____

   _____ .

2. I feel sad when _____

   _____

   _____ .

3. I feel frustrated when _____

   _____

   _____ .

4. I feel scared when _____

   _____

   _____ .

5. I feel angry when _____

   _____

   _____ _____ .

6. I feel proud when _____

   _____

   _____ .

❏ **Activity #14.1: Feelings Picture—Happy**

- Draw a picture of a time when you felt happy.

❑ **Activity #14.2: Feelings Picture—Sad**

- Draw a picture of a time when you felt sad.

❏ **Activity #14.3: Feelings Picture—Frustrated**

• Draw a picture of a time when you felt frustrated.

❏ **Activity #14.4: Feelings Picture—Scared**

- Draw a picture of a time when you felt scared.

❏ **Activity #14.5: Feelings Picture—Angry**

- Draw a picture of a time when you felt angry.

❏ **Activity #14.6: Feelings Picture—Proud**

- Draw a picture of a time when you felt proud.

❏ Activity #15: Flying With Feelings

- Feelings sometimes are connected to color. Color the balloon to match your feelings.

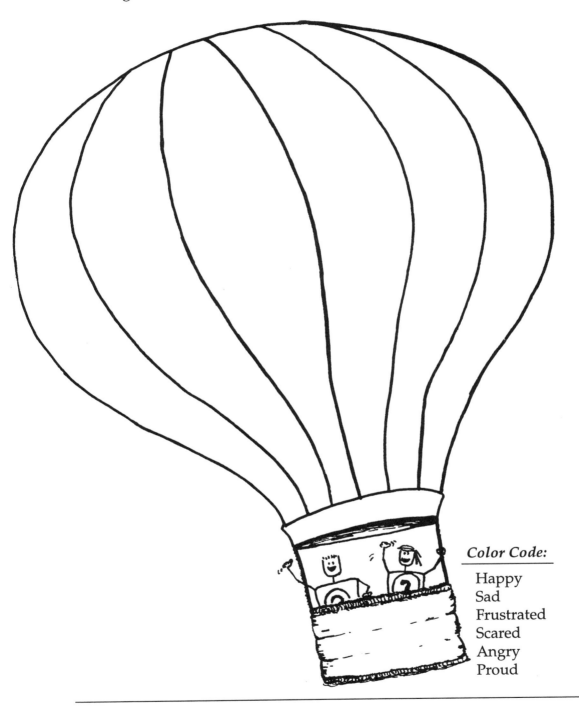

Color Code:

Happy
Sad
Frustrated
Scared
Angry
Proud

4

Boundaries

❑ Message to the Kids

When you were born you, like everyone else, had a special need to be protected and kept safe. People have their own personal space and distance around their bodies that make them feel safe. This is called your *boundary*. Have you ever colored a picture in a coloring book or played a game, like basketball, where you must stay within the lines? These are other examples of boundaries.

When a child is hit, touched in private ways, yelled at, or ignored, his or her boundaries have not been respected. Sometimes people think they are not being respectful only when they have hurt your body, but when they say hurtful things or when they don't take care of your needs, they are still breaking or violating your invisible boundaries.

If someone has hurt you in some way, this probably means you get confused with what is "ok" and "not ok" for people to do. It is important to learn how to keep yourself safe and how to be in control of your actions. This will also allow you to know when others are treating you with respect.

This chapter will help you learn what safe boundaries are, how to keep yourself safe, and how to be safe with others.

❏ **Activity #20: Boundaries—Dot to Dot**

- Connect the dots and color your picture.

❏ **Activity #21: Personal Space**

- Color in the personal space.

❏ **Activity #23: My Personal Space**

- Draw a picture of yourself and color in your personal space.

❑ Activity #24: Shane's Story

- Read or listen to the story and answer the questions.

Shane was having a difficult time. He lived at home with his father and big sister. Shane's father always seemed angry, especially when he was drinking. Now Shane was having problems getting in other people's faces when he was angry. He would yell and push his friends at school.

Shane's teacher was helping him to understand what personal boundaries were and how to respect other people's personal and private space. His teacher would tell him, "When your family has problems with respecting your personal and private space, it is hard to know how to respect others." At home, everybody just did what they wanted without asking. Sometimes, Shane's big sister would just walk in his room to get something without knocking or asking for permission to come in.

Shane now was learning how to use his words to share his feelings. His teacher also was helping him learn how to ask permission before he "borrowed" his friends' things. This all seemed quite confusing to Shane, but he liked the idea of others respecting him and his things. Now he was hoping his family would learn about respecting personal space.

QUESTIONS

1. How did Shane's father and sister violate his boundaries?

   _____

   _____

   _____

   _____

2. How did Shane learn to be more respectful with his friends?

   _____

   _____

   _____

   _____

3. What do you think personal and private space means?

_____

_____

_____

_____

4. Draw a picture of Shane.

❏ **Activity #25: The Private Triangle**

- Look at the picture and practice making your own private triangle with your hands.

❑ **Activity #26: Private Triangle—Dot to Dot**

- Connect the dots and color your picture.

❏ Activity #27: Private Triangle—Cut and Paste

- Cut out the triangle and paste it on the picture, showing where the private triangle should go.

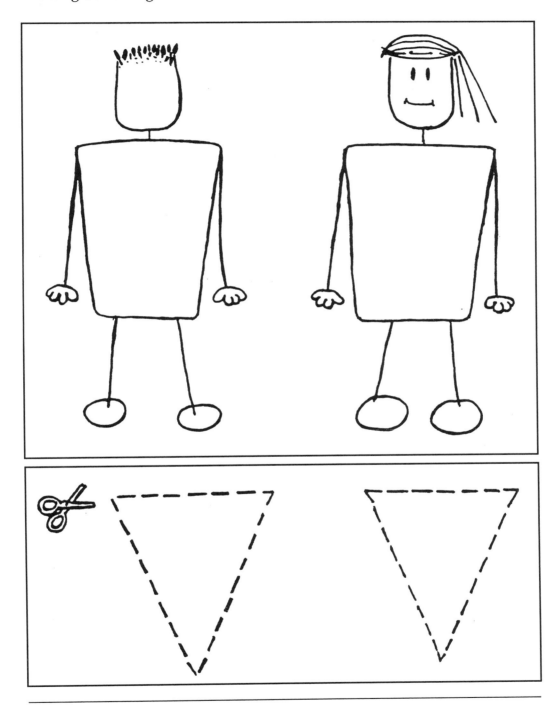

❑ **Activity #28: Private Triangle**

- Draw a picture of yourself and draw in your private triangle.

PHASE II

Exploration of Trauma

5

Developing Trust and Being Safe

❑ **Message to the Kids**

Everybody deserves to feel safe and protected. Kids who have been hurt have had their trust broken. It usually becomes hard to trust others when you haven't been kept safe and protected. It is even sometimes hard to trust yourself when others have hurt you. You may believe it was your fault. You need to know that whatever happened to you WAS NOT YOUR FAULT!

This chapter will help you learn what trust is—how to trust yourself and those people who deserve your trust. You also will learn what being safe means.

❏ **Activity #29: Valerie's Story**

• Read or listen to the story and answer the questions.

Valerie was 7 years old. She lived with her mother in an apartment with her 2-year-old brother, Ruben. Valerie's mother used to like going to the bars with her friends on the weekends. She told Valerie that it was her time to have fun because she worked hard during the week.

There wasn't enough money for baby-sitters and so her mother used to tell Valerie to watch Ruben for her while she went out. Valerie's mother fed Ruben before she left and asked Valerie just to give him his bottle and put him to bed at 8:00 p.m. and then go to bed herself.

Valerie used to be scared at night. Sometimes she heard funny noises and sometimes Mom brought home strange men. They would be laughing and making strange noises in the bedroom, which woke her up. Valerie shared a room with Ruben. She would lie awake and listen, hoping everything was okay.

Sometimes Valerie checked to see if her mom was okay because she heard her crying. One time, Valerie actually saw her mom being hit. This really upset her and she tried to help her mom, but her mom got angry at her and told her to go away. Sometimes Valerie got hit.

Valerie learned not to open her door. On those nights she did not feel very safe. She wanted her mother to tell her everything was okay.

QUESTIONS

1. What does being safe mean to Valerie?

_____

_____

_____

_____

2. What does being safe mean to you?

_____

_____

_____

_____

3. Draw a picture of Valerie.

❑ **Activity #30: My Safe Places**

- Draw or list the places you feel safe.

□ **Activity #31: My Safest Place**

- Write about or draw the place where you feel the safest.

❏ **Activity #32: Unsafe Places**

- List or draw the places you do not feel safe.

❑ **Activity #33: Tommy's Story**

- Read or listen to the story and answer the questions.

Tommy just had his birthday. He was now 10 years old. He was happy he was getting bigger. Still, he was not nearly as big as his brother, Bruce, who was 14 years old. Bruce was really big and used this to get Tommy to do what he wanted him to do.

Tommy hated it when Mom and Dad used to go shopping on the weekends or go to a meeting at school during the week, because Bruce would be left "in charge." Bruce used to make Tommy rake all the leaves in the backyard and clean the dog messes, even though it was his job. If Tommy refused or said he would tell Mom or Dad, Bruce would hit him and threaten to hurt him really bad if he told.

One day, Tommy was tired of always doing what Bruce ordered him to do, so he said "no." Bruce started beating up Tommy. He kept hitting his head on the ground. Tommy had a big bump and bruises on his head. When his parents got home, Bruce said Tommy fell off his bike.

Tommy was afraid to tell. Bruce would always apologize to Tommy, saying he was sorry and that he would never do it again . . . but Bruce always broke his promise.

QUESTIONS

1. Could Tommy trust Bruce in the story? Why?

_____

_____

_____

2. Is there anyone you can trust? Who? Why?

_____

_____

_____

3. What does trust mean to you?

_____

_____

_____

4. Draw a picture of Tommy and Bruce.

❑ **Activity #34: People I Trust**

• Draw a picture of someone you trust. If you want, you can draw more than one person you trust.

❑ **Activity #35: Broken Trust**

- Draw or list different ways trust can be broken.

❏ **Activity #36: People I Don't Trust**

- Draw a picture of a person or people you do not trust.

❑ **Activity #37: Safety Rules**

- Read the following rules to keep yourself safe.

  1. It is ok to say "no" to someone who wants to get in your personal space.

  2. It is ok to express any feeling, as long as you do not hurt anyone or anything.

  3. Keep a safe distance from strangers or people who make you feel uncomfortable.

  List three more ways to keep yourself safe:

  1. _____

  2. _____

  3. _____

6

Secrets

❏ **Message to the Kids**

Surprise! It can be fun to be surprised, like at a surprise birthday party that everyone has kept secret. Fun or safe secrets are fun to keep quiet for a short period of time, like a surprise birthday party.

Difficult or unsafe secrets make you feel "yucky" inside and should not be kept quiet. It's okay to tell someone you trust about the things that make you feel yucky inside.

Many times people who hurt kids tell them "not to tell." Sometimes they will say they will "hurt you, hurt your family, or something terrible will happen." If this has happened to you, it can be very scary to use your words and tell your secret.

It is important for you to know you are worth being kept safe and loved in healthy ways. Telling your secrets is the best way of taking care of yourself.

This chapter will help you learn the difference between safe and unsafe secrets. If you feel safe, you may even be brave enough to use your words and share your scary secrets.

❑ **Activity #38: Samantha's Story**

- Read or listen to the story and answer the questions.

Samantha was 11 years old. She thought she was old enough to go to summer camp like her friends. Instead, her mother told her that she was going to stay with her grandparents again. This made Samantha very upset. She didn't like going there anymore. The summer was a hard time for her mother because her mother and stepfather got divorced. She depended on her parents to watch Samantha and her younger sisters.

Samantha hated leaving the neighborhood where she spent her time playing with her best friend, Jamie, who lived in the same apartment building. She especially hated the "special" times when her grandfather would take her fishing. It was there when he first touched her in her "private places." He told her that it was their "secret" and that no one would believe her if she told. Samantha was confused. She used to like the special times they spent together but wished he would not touch her that way anymore.

As Samantha packed to go to her grandparents, she wondered if her grandfather did anything like that to her mother. She wondered if she should tell her mother. After all, this wasn't a fun secret like Jamie's birthday party.

QUESTIONS

1. What is the difference between safe and unsafe secrets?

_____

_____

_____

_____

2. What was the fun or safe secret in this story?

_____

_____

_____

_____

3. What was the unsafe or difficult secret in this story?

_____

_____

_____

_____

4. What do you think Samantha should do?

_____

_____

_____

_____

❏ **Activity #39: Secrets Make Me Feel . . .**

- Draw or write about how secrets make you feel.

❏ **Activity #40: Safe Places to Share**

- Draw a picture of a place where you feel safe to share difficult secrets.

❏ **Activity #41: I Can Tell!**

- Write about or draw a picture of people you can share your difficult secrets with.

❏ **Activity #42: My Friend's Secret**

- Write a story about a kid who was afraid to tell his or her difficult secret.

Once upon a time _____

_____

_____

_____

_____

_____

_____

_____

_____

_____

_____

_____

_____

_____

_____

_____

_____

The End.

_____

❏ **Activity #43: My Happy Secret**

• Write or draw about a time when you told someone a fun secret.

❑ **Activity #44: My Difficult Secret**

- Write or draw about a time when you told someone a difficult secret.

7

Memories, Nightmares, and "Monsters"

❑ **Message to the Kids**

Remembering everything that has happened is not easy. Remembering can be hard to do because it is painful to think about things you wish didn't happen. Sometimes when things are too scary, you forget or "block" your memories, which might make you think nothing really happened.

Your dreams may be a way of helping you remember scary things. Scary dreams or nightmares are very frightening, but if you let them, they can help you learn more about things that have happened and about your feelings.

Many times children see "monsters" in their scary dreams. This can be very frightening because the monsters seem so real. But the monsters are *not* real.

Your dreams are pictures in your head, like a movie you may have seen. You can learn to have control over your monsters, just like a director has control over a movie being made. The best way to control your "monsters" or direct your scary dreams is to use your words and talk about your thoughts and feelings. Sometimes cartoon "friends" can help solve problems. I bet you have a special cartoon character you feel is powerful and can help you solve problems.

In this chapter, you will learn how to talk about the things you remember and your feelings. If you have scary dreams or nightmares, you will learn new ways to get help. If you have "monsters" that scare you, you will learn how to tame them and be more in charge. Maybe your cartoon "helper" can help you solve problems with monsters.

❏ **Activity #45: I Had a Dream**

- Draw a picture of a dream that you can remember.

❏ **Activity #46: My Happy Dream**

- Draw a picture of a dream that made you happy.

❏ **Activity #47: My Scary Dream**

- Draw a picture of a dream that made you feel scared.

❏ **Activity #48: The Never-Ending Dream**

- Draw a picture of a dream that you had more than once.

❑ **Activity #49: My Monster**

- Draw a picture of your "monster."

❏ **Activity #50: Cartoon Helper**

- Draw a picture of a cartoon helper that can be your "special helper."

❏ **Activity #51: Special Helper to the Rescue!**

- Draw about or list three ways your special helper can help you with your problems.

❏ **Activity #53.1: Important Memories—First Memory**

- Think back to a time when you were very young. Draw a picture of your first memory.

❏ **Activity #53.2: Important Memories—Happiest Memory**

• Draw a picture of your happiest memory.

❏ **Activity #53.3: Important Memories—Saddest Memory**

- Draw a picture of your saddest memory.

❑ **Activity #53.4: Important Memories—Scariest Memory**

• Draw a picture of your scariest memory.

PHASE III

Repairing
the Sense of Self

8

Letting Go of Guilt and Shame

❏ **Message to the Kids**

Everybody wants to be cared for and loved. The problem is that not everyone knows how to show feelings in healthy ways. Sometimes others end up saying or doing hurtful things. It is very confusing when someone you are supposed to be able to trust hurts you instead of keeping you safe.

You may feel like it was your fault when others were hurting you. Their words and actions may make you feel guilty and full of shame. It is not your fault when others make wrong choices and hurt you. The first thing you need to do is to talk about it and realize it was not your fault.

This can be a very sad time for you. You might feel like you have lost out on something because others have hurt you. This might even make you feel like you have "lost" part of being a kid.

You will learn that other people's bad choices were not your fault. You will learn how to talk about your sadness and not feel so guilty. Hopefully, you will be able to learn how to let yourself have fun and not worry so much.

❏ Activity #55: Jay's Story

- Read or listen to the following story and answer the questions.

Jay was so excited the day he finally got a "special friend." Jay lived alone with his mother and big sister. He always wanted a big brother. His mother had filled out all the necessary papers so Jay could join a neighborhood club and become like a little brother to his special friend.

The first outing with Jay's special friend, Ned, was fun. They went miniature golfing. The second time they went swimming at Ned's house. He had such a nice house and his own pool. Because it was now summer, it seemed like they went swimming every week. After about 2 months, Ned suggested they go "skinny-dipping." This felt strange, but Jay thought that because Ned seemed to think it was fun, Jay thought he would try it, too. After all, Ned seemed so great. Everyone really liked him.

Skinny-dipping was kind of fun, but then Ned started leaving "adult" magazines on the bed whenever Jay went over. One day, Ned came in while Jay was drying off and started looking through the magazines. Then he did something that made Jay feel uncomfortable. He asked Jay if he ever "played" with himself. Jay didn't know what to say. Ned then told him he would show him how. He seemed to just want to help Jay, but it seemed strange. Ned assured Jay that it was a fun and normal thing to do.

This became part of the swimming outing every time Jay saw Ned. Now Jay was beginning to feel uncomfortable about going to Ned's. He didn't know what to say. He really liked Ned. Jay also began to feel it was his fault for being willing to go skinny-dipping and look at the magazines with Ned. Now he didn't know what to do.

QUESTIONS

1. Why did Jay think it was his fault?

_____

_____

_____

_____

2. What did Ned tell Jay that made him feel it was ok?

_____

_____

_____

_____

3. Write or draw how you felt after reading the story.

❑ **Activity #57: I Would Say . . .**

* Reread your book and draw a picture of who hurt you and what you would like to say about being hurt.

❑ **Activity #58: Thinking It Was My Fault**

• Complete the following sentences.

1. Sometimes I believe it was my fault because

_____

_____

_____

_____ .

2. Sometimes I believe it was my fault because

_____

_____

_____

_____ .

3. Sometimes I believe it was my fault because

_____

_____

_____

_____ .

4. Sometimes I believe it was my fault because

_____

_____

_____

_____ .

❏ **Activity #59: It Really Wasn't My Fault**

• Read your last sentences and rewrite them in the following sentences.

1. It was not my fault because

_____

_____

_____

_____ .

2. It was not my fault because

_____

_____

_____

_____ .

3. It was not my fault because

_____

_____

_____

_____ .

4. It was not my fault because

_____

_____

_____

_____ .

❑ **Activity #60: Me—Before and After**

- Draw a picture of yourself before you were ever hurt.
- Draw a picture of your "hurt" self.

Before	**After**

❑ **Activity #61: "Lost" Things**

- When children have been hurt, they sometimes feel like they "lost" something. List the things you feel that you have lost:

    1. _____

       _____

    2. _____

       _____

    3. _____

       _____

    4. _____

       _____

    5. _____

       _____

❑ **Activity #62: My Letter**

- Write a letter to your "hurt child."

Dear _____ ,

_____

_____

_____

_____

_____

_____

_____

_____

_____

_____

_____

_____

_____

_____ .

Love,

_____

_____

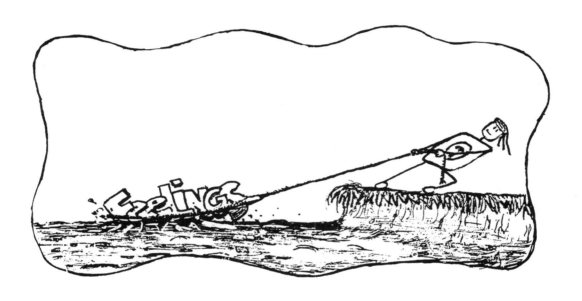

9

Working Through the "Stuck" Feelings

❏ **Message to the Kids**

Congratulations! You have done such a good job. You've talked about so many of your feelings. But you probably still have many other feelings. It is important to talk about these feelings as you start to feel them. You may feel "stuck," but by using your words, you can get "unstuck."

You may start to feel angry at those who hurt you and didn't keep you safe. You also may feel scared about letting your anger out. You can use your words to talk about your feelings so that you don't lose your control.

Kids who won't talk about their angry feelings and who hold them inside can become very sad, blame themselves, and may think about hurting themselves. Sometimes kids feel like hurting others because they are keeping their hurt feelings locked up inside.

In this chapter you will learn how to name and share your feelings in ways that are not hurtful to you or anyone else.

❑ **Activity #63: My Sad Feelings**

- Think about the things that are still causing sad feelings. Then draw a picture or list the things that still make you sad.

- Fill in the "I feel" statements for the things that still cause sad feelings:

  1. I feel sad when _____

  _____ .

  2. I feel sad when _____

  _____ .

  3. I feel sad when _____

  _____ .

  4. I feel sad when _____

  _____ .

❏ **Activity #64: My Scary Feelings**

- Think about the things that are still causing scary feelings. Then draw a picture or list the things that still make you afraid.

```



```

- Fill in the "I feel" statements for the things that still cause scared feelings:

    1. I feel scared when _____

       _____ .

    2. I feel scared when _____

       _____ .

    3. I feel scared when _____

       _____ .

    4. I feel scared when _____

       _____ .

❏ **Activity #65: My Angry Feelings**

• Think about the things that still cause angry feelings. Draw pictures or list the things that still cause angry feelings.

• Fill in the "I feel" statements for the things that still cause angry feelings:

1. I feel angry when _____

_____ .

2. I feel angry when _____

_____ .

3. I feel angry when _____

_____ .

4. I feel angry when _____

_____ .

❏ **Activity #66: Trina's Story**

- Read or listen to the following story and answer the questions.

"Why did you do that?" Trina was so angry that she didn't even notice that when she slammed the door, Ricky was coming in the room and caught the door just before it slammed into him. Trina had such a temper that whenever she was angry, she slammed doors or threw whatever was in her hand at the time. That had gotten her in trouble many times.

Trina felt that no one understood her. She had been through so much. She was now living in a foster home. She was placed there after her teacher noticed the bruises on her arm and began questioning her about them. It wasn't the first time. Her mother had always told her that she deserved it, and she started thinking she did. After all, her father used to beat her mother, and her mother always was apologizing to him for doing something wrong. So Trina started thinking it was her fault every time her mother hit her.

Now Trina's counselor was teaching her how to gain her control. She was working on a book about the different people who hurt her and how she felt about what they did. Now she was learning how to talk about her feelings. She also learned that taking a "time-out" sometimes helped her cool down. Then she could talk about her feelings without throwing things or slamming doors. It was hard. Sometimes her angry feelings just got the best of her . . . like today.

Trina went to her room, opened her journal, and began writing. That was another good way to let out her feelings. She always felt so much better after writing down her feelings. Then she was ready to talk about what was frustrating her.

QUESTIONS

1. What were the unhealthy ways Trina took care of anger?

_____

_____

_____

_____

_____

2. What were the healthy ways Trina took care of anger?

_____

_____

_____

_____

3. What are healthy ways you can take care of your anger?

_____

_____

_____

_____

❏ **Activity #67: My Contract**

- Complete the following contract.

  I will take care of my angry, hurt, and sad feelings by:

  _____

  _____

  _____

  _____

  _____

  _____

  _____

  _____

  _____

  _____

  _____

  _____

  Signed by _____

  _____

❏ **Activity #68: Beginning My Journal**

• Write about your thoughts and feelings today.

Today I am feeling

_____

_____

_____

_____

_____

_____

_____

_____

_____

_____

_____

_____

_____

_____

❏ **Activity #69: You Hurt Me!**

- Write a letter to someone who hurt you. Make sure you tell how you felt about what that person did to hurt you.

To: _____

_____

_____

_____

_____

_____

_____

_____

_____

_____

_____

_____

_____

_____

Signed by _____

_____

PHASE IV

Becoming Future Oriented

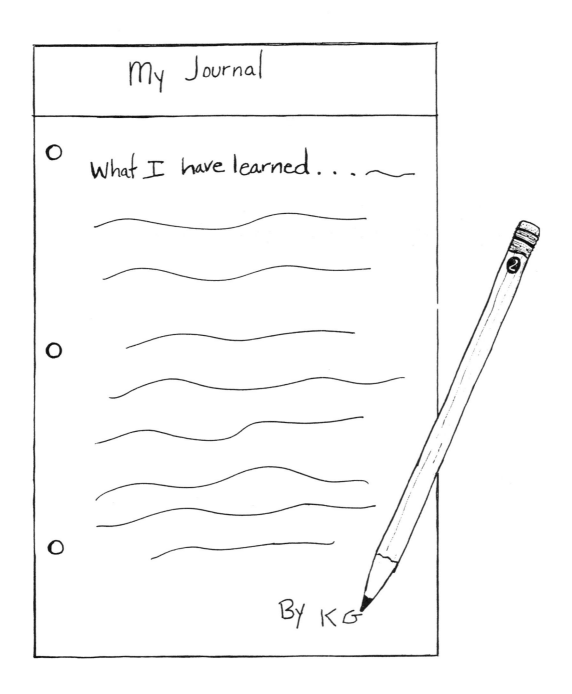

10

What Have I Learned?

❏ **Message to the Kids**

You've done a great job! You have learned how to name and talk about your feelings in ways that are not hurtful to you or others. You know more about safe boundaries and how to protect your personal space. You have learned what trust is and what being safe means. You have learned the difference between safe and unsafe secrets.

You have worked on how to talk about your memories and the feelings that go along with them. You have learned that your dreams can sometimes help with your memories. You have also learned how to "tame" your monster.

You have learned that you are not responsible for other people's bad choices when they hurt you. You also have learned how to use your words to let out your angry and hurt feelings.

Wow, you really have learned a lot! But healing your hurt feelings takes time. You can't always make your hurt go away as fast as you may want. This chapter will help you decide how much you have learned and what things you still need to work on.

❑ **Activity #70: Pride List**

- After all of the work you have done, you have a lot to be proud of. Write or draw the things that make you feel proud.

❏ **Activity #71: I Am Special!**

- Write or draw the things you like about yourself.

❏ **Activity #72: Things I've Learned**

- Write about the things you have learned.

❏ **Activity #73: Me Today!**

- Draw a picture of who you are now.

Appendix

❏ **Parental Guidance and Sexual Development**

Parental guidance is crucial in children's development

Parents give values about sexuality

Sex can be associated with shame and/or guilt if parents:
- View sex as dirty, inapprorpriate or secretive
- Set rigid and restrictive limits on healthy curiosity, self-exploration, and questions
- Punish, chastise, or humiliate children for appropriate sexual exploration

Parents being oversexualized in front of children may create a sexualized environment. This may include the following:
- Highly sexual behaviors
- Adult nudity/pornographic material
- Lack of appropriate boundaries

Parents being undersexualized in front of children may give the message that sex is taboo. This may include the following:
- Adults never being physically affectionate
- Parents never allowing healthy sexual questions

Parents can provide a healthy environment by:
- Being openly affectionate without becoming overly sexualized
- Teaching children and providing an atmosphere in which children feel comfortable that asking questions is ok

Child Abuse Trauma Interview (CATI)

Child's Name: _____

DOB: _____ Chronological Age: _____

Primary Therapist: _____

Interviewer: _____ Date of Interview: _____

Background Information

1. Are your birth parents married, single, separated, or divorced?

   _____

2. Who do you live with? _____

   If not with birth parents, why? _____

   _____

3. List siblings, including ages: _____

   _____

4. Did you ever live with someone other than your mom or dad?

   yes _____   no _____

   If yes, with whom? (include ages and dates): _____

   _____

5. Have you ever been in trouble with the police?

   yes _____   no _____

   If yes, describe: _____

   _____

   _____

6. Have you ever used alcohol or other drugs (AOD)?

   yes _____   no _____

   Describe: _____

   _____

   _____

7. Have either of your parents had problems with alcohol or other drugs
   (AOD)? yes _____   no _____

   If yes, what? _____

   _____

   _____

8. Did the AODs cause any problems? yes _____   no _____

   If so, what? _____

   _____

   _____

   _____

9. Did you ever see one parent hit or beat up the other parent or a sibling?

   yes _____   no _____

   If yes, describe what happened: _____

   _____

   _____

   _____

Psychological/Emotional Maltreatment

Have you ever experienced any of the following? If so, how often?

(include notation of who)	Never	Sometimes	Lots of times	Most of the time
1. Yelled at you	0	1	2	3
2. Called you names	0	1	2	3
3. Made you feel guilty	0	1	2	3
4. Made fun of you	0	1	2	3
5. Embarrassed you in front of others	0	1	2	3
6. Made you feel like you were a bad person	0	1	2	3
7. "Silent treatment"	0	1	2	3
8. Locked you in a room, closet, or other small space	0	1	2	3
9. Tied you or chained you to something	0	1	2	3
10. Threatened to hurt or kill you	0	1	2	3
11. Threatened to hurt or kill someone you care about	0	1	2	3
12. Threatened to hurt or kill your pet	0	1	2	3
13. Threatened to leave you somewhere	0	1	2	3
14. Threatened to leave and never come back	0	1	2	3
15. Other: _____	0	1	2	3

16. Was Child Protective Services or the police ever called?

   yes _____   no _____

   If yes, what happened? _____

   _____

   _____

17. Did you ever see a doctor for your injuries? _____ yes _____ no

    If yes, describe: _____

    _____

Physical Maltreatment

Have you ever experienced any of the following? If so, how often?

	Never	Sometimes	Lots of times	Most of the time
(include notation of who)				
1. Spanked	0	1	2	3
2. Hit/slapped	0	1	2	3
3. Punched	0	1	2	3
4. Pulled hair	0	1	2	3
5. Scratched	0	1	2	3
6. Twisted arm	0	1	2	3
7. Pushed	0	1	2	3
8. Banged head	0	1	2	3
9. Attempted drowning	0	1	2	3
10. Broken bones or teeth	0	1	2	3
11. Bruises	0	1	2	3
12. Bleeding	0	1	2	3
13. Other _____	0	1	2	3

14. Was Child Protective Services or police ever called?

    _____ yes _____ no

    If yes, what happened? _____

    _____

15. Did you ever need to see a doctor for your injuries?

    _____ yes _____ no

    If yes, describe: _____

    _____

    _____

Sexual Maltreatment

1. Has anyone ever kissed you in a way that made you feel
   uncomfortable? _____ yes _____ no

   If yes, indicate who: _____

   _____

   Describe what happened (include ages and number of times):

   _____

   _____

   _____

   Did anyone ever make you kiss him or her?

   _____ yes _____ no

   If yes, who? _____

   _____

2. Have you ever seen or been made to look at movies, magazines,
   pictures, etc. of private touching? _____ yes _____ no

   If yes, describe: _____

   _____

3. Has anyone ever showed you his or her private parts or made you
   take off your clothes in front of that person?

   _____ yes _____ no

   If yes, who (include ages)? _____

   _____

Describe what happened (include ages and number of times):

_____

_____

_____

4. Has anyone ever touched your body in a way that made you feel uncomfortable? _____ yes _____ no

   If yes, who? _____

   _____

   Describe what happened (include ages and number of times):

   _____

   _____

5. Has anyone ever made you touch him or her in a way that made you feel uncomfortable? _____ yes _____ no

   If yes, indicate who (include ages): _____

   _____

   Describe what happened (include ages and number of times):

   _____

   _____

   _____

6. Has anyone ever put anything in your private parts?

   _____ yes _____ no

   If yes, who did this? _____

   _____

Describe what happened (include ages and number of times):

_____

_____

_____

7. Has anyone ever put any part of his or her body in your private parts?

    _____ yes _____ no

   If yes, who did this? _____

   Describe what happened (include ages and number of times):

   _____

   _____

   _____

8. Has anyone ever touched your private parts with his or her mouth or made you touch his or her private parts with your mouth?

    _____ yes _____ no

   If yes, who? _____

   Describe what happened: _____

   _____

   _____

   _____

9. Was Child Protective Services ever called because of the private touching? _____ yes _____ no

   If yes, describe (include dates or age at time): _____

   _____

   _____

10. Have you ever touched someone in a way that made that person feel uncomfortable? _____ yes _____ no

   If yes, describe what happened: _____

   _____

   _____

   _____

11. Additional information: _____

   _____

   _____

   _____

   _____